O'Africa

Volume I   A POETRY COLLECTION

P. Carol Johnson

Ingram Sparks

Contents

DEDICATION

O' AFRICA IS DEDICATED to Carol Denise Johnson, a woman of unparalleled strength, beauty, and grace whose imprint on my life has shaped me into the woman I am. Aunt Carol, my Divine, you are always with me.

CAROL DENISE JOHNSON

FORWARD

T HERE ARE MOMENTS IN literature when words do more than document—they resurrect. They reach back into the deepest recesses of memory, binding the past to the present, ensuring that what has been lived is neither forgotten nor misplaced in history's unrelenting march forward. *O' Africa, Volume 1* is one such collection. It does not merely exist within the realm of poetry—it breathes, it calls, it recalls.

This collection is the beating heart of an ancestral journey, a meditation on lineage and survival, framed through verse that unearths both **historical recall and belongingness**—two forces that shape the African American experience. Within these pages, the James family emerges not just as historical figures but as **symbols of an enduring thread.** A thread that stretches from the toil of sharecropping in South Carolina, to the triumphs and complexities of contemporary Black existence in the United States.

At the center of this poetic journey is the Sankofa bird—its gaze fixed backward, its wings poised forward. It is a deliberate act of remembrance, a refusal to move ahead without first gathering the wisdom left behind by those who paved the way. Here, the *elders speak*, their voices woven into a tapestry of hard-earned wisdom, labor, sacrifice, and quiet victories. Their names—like **James Johnson, Chizzie James, Edmond James, and Carol Denise Johnson**—resonate throughout the collection, echoing across generations, refusing erasure.

In many ways, this work is more than a poetic tribute—it is a ***gravitational force,*** pulling the reader into its orbit, demanding an emotional reckoning with the weight of history. It is impossible to read these poems without feeling the presence of those who came before—those who labored under the scorching sun of the South, who carved communities from nothing, who held fast to dignity even in the face of systemic erasure.

Yet, this is not just a story of endurance—it is a story of ***interconnection, movement, and rebirth***. Each poem serves as both ***testament and invitation***, urging the reader to recognize the continuum of history, not as something distant, but as something alive in the choices, struggles, and triumphs of today's generations. The significance of family, the unbreakable ties to a South Carolina home and community, the unwavering belief in one's place within a larger African lineage—all of these elements make *O' Africa* not just personal, but deeply collective.

Part I calls forth a challenge—to bridge divisions and reclaim dignity in the face of fragmentation. ***Part II*** traces the ***James lineage,*** revealing the poets, prophets, and builders of a legacy whose names remain etched into time. ***Part III*** stands as both closure and beginning, leading toward ***Volume II,*** where the echoes of ***Carol Denise Johnson*** usher in new voices, new storytellers, new keepers of the ancestral flame.

This is the poetry of reclamation. This is the poetry of knowing. This is *O' Africa*, where history refuses to fade, where memory insists on being carried, and where the past, no matter how distant, remains tethered to the future.

Dr. Lindelwa Ntutela

PREFACE

THIS COLLECTION EXPLORES HISTORICAL knowledge, illuminates the past, and explains the present. It captures elements of our Pan African family history going back to the connectedness of Ervin James' clan to slavery in the South. It further brings our history and lived experiences forward to the timeline of Phillip and Lazurah, two young men coming of age in the first quarter of the 21st century.

In a ground-breaking book, *The Fourth Turning: An American Prophecy,* authors Strauss and Howe (1997) have posited that archetypes are identifiable in each generation - the Hero, the Artist, the Prophet, and the Nomad. Each consists of people born in a roughly twenty-year period. As each archetypal generation reaches the end of its lifespan, the cycle repeats. A new hero, artist, prophet, or nomad is born.

While these archetypal forms are palpable, the pattern that describes generations of the James family is grounded, and in turn grounds and anchors its members in continental Africa, following the Ghanaian concept of Sankofa that roots us in the greater African family. Reading between the lines, the poems in this collection point out to the reader the heroes, artists, prophets, and nomads. Sometimes a single poem may contain or show the presence of two or three archetypes in one. What is clear is that our history tells the story of an interconnected and multigenerational web of relatives: of an African family's rendezvous with destiny. The collection does not follow a linear pattern. It derives structure from the Sankofa essence and spirit, which states that we should reach back and gather the best of what our past has to teach us so that we can achieve our full potential as we move forward. Whatever we have lost, forgotten, foregone, or been stripped of can be reclaimed, revived, preserved, and perpetuated.

This spirit has connected generations of my family. We have dug the trench holes of slavery, experienced the betrayals and triumphs of share-cropping, witnessed the strange fruit of Jim Crow, fought and lived through American and world wars, and survived the ravages of epidemics, including the two contemporary pandemics of COVID-19 and social justice. Older generations have exited honorably, leaving new heroes, artists, prophets, and nomads who continue to cultivate a support system that has kept the James legacy intact. As the Sankofa bird's head faces backwards, it symbolizes for us the knowledge of the past and signifies the generations that come to benefit from that wisdom. The egg itself symbolizes new life, a rebirth made possible through individual and collective forgiveness, healing, correcting, revising, deconstructing, and reclaiming what we have been stripped of or lost, and preserving what new generations must perpetuate.

Part I is a *Call* to Action that expresses the urgency to transcend the divisions of language and culture that separate us in our workspaces, our places of worship, institutions of higher learning, and our communities. At a time when discourse about multiculturalism is at the top of the agenda in every nation state, we make the assertion that it is possible to move forward, restore and reclaim the trust and dignity we lost as our African families were separated through the Middle Passage, even as we share collectively, our memories of slavery, colonialism and continue to fight for the eradication of structural inequality and systemic racism throughout the diasporic world.

Part II, My African Family, explores the cast of characters in the James family lineage, beginning with Chizzie James, granddaughter of Ervin James. Chizzie James was born on December 6th, 1904, following Reconstruction in the South. She was raised and educated not past the 5th grade in Little River, South Carolina. Although she could not read, Chizzie mastered animal husbandry, baking, bookkeeping, and homemaking. Chizzie would marry Edmond James of Black Creek, a World War 1 veteran. Together, they began their family in segregated Florence, South Carolina. Just as Chizzie and Edmond's ancestors survived slavery and triumphed in the face of Reconstruction and Jim Crow, so too would the descendants of Chizzie and Edmond James.

We close **Part II** with a brief history that ties the heroes, prophets, artists, and nomads of the James tribe together through narrative. As my great, great grandmother, Chizzie James, the prophet of the James family, faced the end of life at eighty, a child was born, Philadelphia Iña Paul. She knew this child was the one, the last great-grandchild that she would raise, and the one in whom she could instill the teachings, history, and essence of the James family. Orally, Chizzie James recounted the history of her people and how we came to be, as Philadelphia ardently listened. She said, *"Now you listen, chile, cause I ain't gonna be here much longer. You need to know who you are and never forget."* I am that child, and this is our story, *O' Africa*.

Part III is a bridge to *Volume II*. As the final verse of the poetry collection finds its rest, we stand at the threshold of reminiscence and revelation. *Part III* serves as a reflective closure to our poetry collection. It also provides a narrative link to an upcoming memoir, born of the felt need to honor a departed, central figure in our lives, an influential businesswoman and intergenerational leader who carried the torch of contemporary history in the James family. In November 2023, as the ink dried in the writing process, Carol Denise Johnson passed on to be with the Lord. She had curated some of the poetry and had the manuscript read out loud to her in her final days. Now, as younger generations prepare to step into her shoes, a new volume of work, a memoir, emerges that breathes life into this beloved matriarch whose whispers have accompanied our poetic odyssey and our lives.

PART 1

A CALL TO ACTION

O' AFRICA

O H AFRICA
The source of all creation
The Rosetta Stone of all languages
The riches upon which our world would be built

Oh Africa
Your most precious treasure was torn away from you
like all of your treasures
Your children

Oh Africa
Plunder for Africa and all of its people
Murdered, Raped, Kidnapped en masse
Taken away by the sword
Genocide
Taken to all parts of the world
Fractured
Brother separated from sister

Babies ripped apart whilst still suckling on their mother's breasts
Never to be seen again
Jamaica, Puerto Rico, Cuba, Brazil, the Americas, Europe, Asia
Generations lost to you
Each survivor lost
Indefinitely
Separated from you
Our Motherland

Oh Africa
Oh Africa
Oh Africa
We are here
The lost children of Africa
Together we are Africa

O' AFRICA

YOU CALLED ME BY NAME

F ROM THE MOMENT I saw you
Incarnation of God in Man
Regal in stature
Beauty that leaves me spellbound
Thick lips
High cheekbones
Skin the color of the African midnight sky from which you came
Eyes sparkling like stars
I just want to be near

I run to the beat of the music the minstrels play, announcing your arrival
King
My beautiful African king
I love you
With anyone else, I would be less than a Queen
No other compares
Your worth is beyond gold or any measure of man
Your touch

Only in your arms do I discover heaven on earth, paradise

Years passed, so many years
The memory of being exalted in your
majestic presence never fades
The glow of your spirit
Like a light beckoning me to stand at your side
Speaking life into the abyss of the world's chaos
Like the prophet for whom you called
You bring out the light

With you, I don't need a title
Wife, girlfriend, partner
Should you call me, call me
I don't know who you saw when you met me all those years ago
I hope the next time you see me, and our eyes meet,
you see me for who I am, yours
The only title I've had or should ever aspire to be

Your woman
Your queen, honored to be yours

OCEAN BREEZE

YOU CALLED ME BY name
    Now I answer to only you
You called me by name
Now I answer to only you

You called me by name
Now I answer to only you
Life began in your arms
In your eyes, I saw my future unfold
My hand in yours, I found security and safety for the first time
Though oceans keep us apart
Always we are together in my heart

You called me by name
Now I answer to only you
Feet surrounded by sand
Every muscle relaxes
Engulfed by an ocean breeze

In this moment, I feel you here with me
I smell you in the wind
Your body's natural fragrance blends with the salt, sea, and sand
Floating away with you is heavenly

Your hand in mine
A gentle touch is all it takes to take me there with you
Though my eyes are closed
I can see your face forming in ocean waves
This sacred space is filled with your energy

You are everywhere
Though we are apart
We are so connected
Distance could never divide you and me
You called me by name
Now I answer to only you

I am only what I answer to
Yours

OCEAN BREEZE

RICHMOND

S OMETIMES I WANT TO call you

But I won't

Sometimes I want to write you

But this pen won't let me

Then I want to give you my heart

But your heart won't accept me

Sometimes I'll miss your light and your smile

The way you kiss me lightly and your simple style

Then I'll give you that gift that you can't receive

But I can't get back

So, I'll simply ask

Are you happy here?

Knowing you're alone on your path

But there is someone out there

Just as the speed of light delivers the stars' bright gleam

Defy the boundaries of time

So, does my heart, seeking your own

So, I ask you
Are you happy in her arms of artifice
The duplicate and representative of selfish insecurity
When you could just as easily delve into a sea of the alluring me
But are you happy?

Star gazing in the early morning light
Thinking about you, and I saw him
There on a corner
My future is in his eyes
As I stared at my tomorrow's end
In the depths of his round brown portals
Illuminated by beautiful brown skin
I thought of you and how

Sometimes I want to call you
But I won't
Sometimes I want to write you
But this pen won't let me
Then I want to give you my heart
But your heart won't accept me
Sometimes I'll miss your light and your smile
The way you kiss me lightly and your simple style
Then I'll give you that gift that you can't receive
But I can't get back
So, I'll simply ask
Are you happy here?

Then I come back to this stranger

The one on the corner with my tomorrow's end in his eyes
His beautiful brown skin wrapped around his piece
Not his peace like wisdom or positive energy,
which always causes elevation
But piece, be steel in his hands
Hard steel, just like hard love
So there

I'm on the corner as this steel faces my chest
He says, Give me all your money, your body, strip for me
I said, Stranger, I don't have anything to give, I'm empty
Just turn around and strip for me, and I'll spare your life
Hey stranger, I know I see my tomorrow's end in your eyes
But I know what you don't
I am an empty vessel of the Most High
I will not give you what is his

So just kill me
Take my body
Take it
Cause I ain't got nothing to give to you tonight
Look, just turn around
Turn that bag of yours upside down
Strip for me and I'll spare your life

Sorry, stranger, I know what you don't
It's all or nothing, so if you're taking anything tonight
Then take it all
That's when those illuminating round brown eyes stared

at his piece be steel, and he cocked it, and I thought

Sometimes I want to call you
But I won't
Sometimes I want to write you
But this pen won't let me
Then I want to give you my heart
But your heart won't accept me
Sometimes I'll miss your light and your smile
The way you kiss me lightly and your simple style
Then I'll give you that gift that you can't receive
But I can't get back
So, I'll simply ask
Are you happy here?

Here I am bleeding to death in this alley all alone
Left
All or nothing
So, I gave him all I owned, nothing now it's too late
I hoped you answered yes
I'm happy

MIDNIGHT

MIDNIGHT
      Gentle firm undeniable
Fully present
Around me
Your aura fills my spirit
Sending sensations down my spine and through my body
Your touch
Pulls me back to this moment

Better late than never
Your eyes weigh into me
Pulling me into this place
Midnight
I can't stay here
Because dawn will come
You were never really mine
But for a moment at midnight
I lived a fantasy

Where you were mine
Your energy is a part of me
Your body and mine
Intertwined
Your eyes that have always seen me as I am, completely
As no one else has
Your skin...midnight

Though I know you belong to the dawn
I live for the moment
The hour of midnight
In the darkness that allows
You and I to be
Like vapor
In the midst of your heat, the fog that conceals our love fades
Hmm...I saw the bright light of infinity reflected from your ring
And I know that on some level
You and I belong together

But you will never be mine
Dawn will always have her day
But if only in our dreams
You and I will be together always
Always
At midnight

MAGNETISM

WHY ARE YOU AFRAID of me?
    You hold onto your fear
Your fear that you can no longer control
Stop yourself from loving
From giving your body completely
From giving in to this feeling that is more spiritual than emotional

Let go and go with it
To a place that your control
Your identity cannot breach
I felt it
I knew the first time I saw you
I could no more walk away from you
Than walk away from life

Before I touched you
I knew your skin
Before I kissed you

I knew your taste
Before we crossed the thin line that separated you from me
I knew we weren't a you and I
But one entity

Beautifully blended
I have only been waiting for you
To give in and let go
Of the lie that you live outside of this thing between us
I know you better than anyone knows you, and I know you want me
Your body stands at attention when I walk into the room
Everything inside of you responds to me

Can you deny this?
Your hands are reaching out to embrace me
Your body longs for the touch of my hands
Only in my arms will you find peace from this
You have convinced yourself that when you walk out of here
That you will regain control of your senses

You believe this is a fluke
You close your eyes so that you don't see
The promise in my own
The promise of what our love will be
The culmination of everything we have been tiptoeing around
Passion, Desire, visceral Need, love

The truth is, when you leave
I will go with you

When you close your eyes
I am always with you
The memories of our love
Your eyes following the rise and fall of my breasts
The heat running between our bodies
Sealing
Binding us together
Your mouth demanding kissing and licking down my neck
I see the impact of the memories as they wash over you

Standing in your denial
Your scent
Your scent is in the air
I inhale once more just to be sure
Yes, your scent
Without saying a word
You tell me everything I need to know
You need me
You want me
Your body is yearning to find fulfillment;
the only way fulfillment can be found

CORAL STONE

CORAL STONE
Coral shell
Embedded coral shell
As she fell between the crumpled cracks of your sheets
Enveloped
Two beating hearts consumed
By the passions of their carnal flesh
Now I lie consumed by the waters
The holy waters abound

Flesh and blood
Humanity will only go so far
Good works inspired by good words
Something greater than thy idol worshipping
Mystery of iniquity
Now I fully understand
The unspoken word
The words that live in the silence and tears when we two parted

What does it really mean to love?
Floating on the currents of your water
Delving into my passion
Blowing in the wind
Ashes

Drowning in the blurring depths of the sea
Consuming what I seek in my sea of denial
Delving into my pain for the love of the flesh
Scattered on the forgotten nation
Ashes
Time no longer limits the reality I know
Embracing
As trees take motion with free breeze
Birds in flight
Rain descends
But time
Time will stop as my heart

So does the spirit
Wrapped around my body
Consumed in the currents
Descending beyond the waters
Into the ocean's floor
Now I see coral flowing with the currents of your waters

Stung like a serpent on land
But now it ascends thorns
Rising above the cobblestone road

Held in the bondage of your love
My spirit
As my eyes looked
Coral stone wind chimes
Molded into mystic triangles, creating the loudest unheard sound
Of freedom distorted
My ears are open
My eyes are too
I thought as I closed the cobblestone door of my heart
for the very last time

CORAL STONE

COLORS OF LIFE

S HADES OF PINK AND purple dance across the horizon
   As a cool breeze blows by, warm and sweet
A reward from the toilsome days of late
A beautiful day, almost eerie
This is a New England November day
The pain I harvested in the dying fields of my heart
Created by some foreign creature
So villainous, who but you would steal all that is left of me
My solace

This ache flows through the rivers of my mind
Time drained those rivers
A smile steals what once reflected me
A portion of my face looks new and revitalized
As if you that had condemned me
Breathed new air into my lungs
Forgiveness

But no
For that, I cannot credit you
Yesterday, someone asked me
Who is your father
I replied, I do not know this man
Today, I know that no earthly being can ever redeem me
as my Father in heaven
But your name is not hallowed

Everyone is chasing the almighty dollar
Nothing is sacred
Integrity is sold
My heart is scorned so deeply
The pain has seared through my being wholly completely
All for some form of wickedness
Now, as I admire the pink and purple shades of the damning sky
I enjoy the last days in which we live
I cannot differentiate the seasons nor man from deceit
I embrace my love and accept myself
Unconditionally, in my thirst for such love
I met iniquity

It sought me out and wanted to feel the beating of my heart
Explore its inner chambers
Now, as I look at the pink and purple of my flesh
I hurt
The idea that man could be so violent towards woman
Kills the fertility of love, the sacred ankh
But those colors are not so visible on my flesh

but rather on the canvas of my heart

COLORS OF LIFE

OBSCURITY

I KNOW YOU'RE UP there
　　Somewhere beyond the blues and blacks
Your aura runs through me
Connected
Filling me so completely
I need to be filled
Hmm, fill me with your light

Why can't I see your light?
Beyond the darkness
Beyond the blues and blacks of the night sky
I feel a thump, thump, thump
Fighting and pushing away from the blues and blacks

Towards the beautiful brown
Brown surfaces
So scarred and so bruised
Why can't I feel it filling me

My eyes with your light
Why can't I see your light?

Please move towards the horizon
Toward the beautiful bronze sun beyond
Move towards the light
So, I might see you in the day

Hold your hand
Feel your spirit
Fill me with your light
Feel your heart

Thump, thump, thump
The portals of my soul are overflowing
The blues and blacks are clouding my vision

Can't see beyond
Can't feel beyond the pain
Why
Please fight
Where is the light?

STEPPING STONE

THE DEVIL WALKS AMONG US

    Shh, it could be you

The purest form of grace

But I covered your brown with white face

That way, I could pretend you died a martyr

The greatest sacrifice for the noblest of causes

You see, I could change the world with just one more opportunity

With your meek little shoulders as steps

I could step on and rise to greatness and power

Now the only stone there is

Lay six feet under my soul

The devil walks among us

Among you and me

Perhaps just as I denied the God in you

Maybe it is the devil which runs through me

God's amazing works

For you are the purest form of grace
For which I had no mercy
Now, as I visualize how your eyes were
I see what you saw
My eyes in your eyes

Concrete
I stepped on your fragile heart and watched it break
Crumbling before my eyes
I realized
My eyes had turned cold
Just as your eyes turned stone
Stone
Your gravestone
Six feet under my soul

You had my eyes and God's purest form of grace
He gave your love unto me
Yet I easily replaced you
With steps and a solid path leading to success

The devil walks among us
He lived in me
He thrived in me
Now, as I realize my dreams
My greatness and my success
I see I lost God's purest form of grace

STEPPING STONE

PART II

O' AFRICA: MY AFRICAN FAMILY

MARY CHIZZIE JAMES

C HIZZIE JAMES
      Africa
The People
Child of Jim Crow
Daughter of Jamestown

You endured the indignity
Of second-class citizenry
Shuffled off the sidewalks
Of segregated Florence
Gave up your seat
Swallowed the shame of degradation
All for the survival of your lineage

Our DNA
The cornerstone of our identity
It was your blood
Your sweat

Your tears
That gave us life
You are the foundation of our family
Our direct connection to Africa
And to our ancestors

Like the stars in the night sky
Illuminating our way forward
You're always there
We only have to look up
Look in

You are with us
The soil beneath our feet
The ocean breeze blowing by
The rain falling down
The morning midst rising from the mountains
You are the cardinal
Flying outside my window
You are
The hydrangeas in spring
Now you are everywhere

Giver of our blessings, our purpose
The strongest thread seamlessly woven
Between five generations
Locking us together

You were the one who said

"Baby, there's a song
That only you can sing
Oh, how it needs to be heard."
That song is ***O' Africa***
I sing for you

BELOVED MARY

Beloved Mary Elaine Scott

"AND," MARY SAID, *"My soul doth magnify the Lord, And my spirit hath rejoiced in God my Savior, For he hath regarded the low estate of his handmaiden: for, behold, from henceforth all generations shall call me blessed."*

A woman of distinction.

A Proverbs 31 woman, who, like Naomi of Judah, in the wake of the bitter loss of your sisters, Ruth and Edna Mae, took the children left behind unto your bosom.

All while raising your devoted daughter, Penni.

Like Esther of ShuShan, she led the family through the storm with prayer, determination, and wisdom.

Like Mary of a certain village, clave unto your sister, Martha, and nurtured the covenant of sisterhood all the days of your life, creating a legacy of black unity and excellence so few families are afforded.

Though we now face the swift darkness of grief, you, Mary Elaine Scott, will continue to be a source of light in all of our lives.

You are here with us, telling us we must hold on to your light. We must follow your shining example of a humble woman of God. A woman of God whose every word, every gentle touch, every sacrifice, every joy, and every day given in service to the least of these magnified the Lord.

Therefore, we know that this is not goodbye because you are with the Lord in that special place he has prepared for you.

Like Naomi of Jerusalem, Esther of Shushan, and Mary of Bethany, we will never forget our beloved Mary Elaine Scott of Florence, South Carolina.

"Now it came to pass, as they went, that he entered into a certain village: and a certain woman named Martha received him into her house. And she had a sister called Mary, which also sat at Jesus' feet, and heard his word."

"But Martha was cumbered about much serving, and came to him, and said, Lord, dost thou not care that my sister hath left me to serve alone? Bid her therefore that she help me."

"And Jesus answered and said unto her, Martha, Martha, thou art careful and troubled about many things: But one thing is needful: and Mary hath chosen that good part, which shall not be taken away from her."

We love you, Mary Elaine Scott. You will live forever in our hearts. Rest in Power.

(Luk. 1.46-48,10.38-42)

MARY JAMES SCOTT

MARTHA'S HANDS

"*And let the beauty of the Lord our God be upon us: and establish thou the work of our hands upon us; yea, the work of our hands, establish thou it.*"

Martha's hands gently nurtured, cleaned, bathed, fed, four generations of children, nieces, nephews, grandchildren, and great-grandchildren, starting with her own two.

As those young men and women faced a cold world. Martha's hands kept a door open, a hot meal, a warm welcome, and words of wisdom ready to guide, teach, and lead the way.

Martha's hands faithfully held Eugene's for over half a century.

When the ashes of death fell upon our family, taking her sisters Ruth and Edna Mae, Martha's hands embraced their children. Martha, along with her twin-sister Mary, kept God's promise in Isaiah to Bestow on them a crown of beauty instead of ashes, the oil of joy instead of mourning, and a garment of praise instead of a spirit of despair.

Martha's hands wiped their tears, healed their hurts, and bestowed upon all of her children a glorious headdress.

A Proverbs 31 woman, Martha put her hands to the distaff and on the spindle to provide, stitch, knit, and design, ensuring that all of her children were clothed in strength and dignity.

As Martha's hands now fade from our physical realm, we take solace knowing that Martha's hands are now holding the hands that held hers for 89 and a half years, her twin sister Mary.

Jesus said unto her, *"Martha, I am the resurrection, and the life; he that believeth in me, though he were dead, yet shall he live. And whosoever believeth in me shall never die. Believest thou this, Martha?"* Martha saith unto him, *"Yes, Lord, I believe that art the Christ, the son of God, which should come into the world."* When Martha had said so, she went her way.

Martha Renetta James Whack, we love you. We always will. Thank the Lord our God for the work of your hands.

(Isa. 61:1-3, Prv. 31:19, Jhn. 11:25-28)

MARTHA RENETTA JAMES WHACK

ELDER

T HE ELDER IN THE village who raised me
    A man of few words
But many values

Your work ethic hearkens back to the days of our ancestors
Tirelessly working to establish and maintain Jamestown
Your will to work, since the age of thirteen
Defies even the limitations of human form

Back home
They called him ***"Kid"*** because he was so smooth
Class of 1977

Killing them on the court
Most Valuable Player
Three years running
Undefeated
Representing good ole Wilson High

The best
Better than all the rest

Keeper of our rituals
Our recipes
Our rites of passage
Role model for the next generation

Man of unparalleled style and dignity
He lives Second Thessalonians
"If a man will not work, he will not eat."
Hungry to feed his family

Sunday dinners every Sunday
Thanksgivings, Christmas, birthdays
Family man
Faithful and loyal husband of thirty-one years
Honored at his coming in and his goings out

I will always cherish our family vacations, high rolling
You have taught me so much more than how to play the numbers
You taught me how to push through the pain to live to fight another day
You taught me to find joy in the garden

You taught me much of our rich history
My favorite uncle on both sides is
Striking
Reserved yet witty
His grin contagious

If he calls you a friend, you are a friend for life
Loyal to a fault
Silently standing ten toes down in his truth
Always willing to help anyone in need
A good man
He is the best of men

PAPI

No horse
    No carriage
What I did have was the best view of Florence
from the top of your shoulders
Where I sat for the first five years of my life

Looking down
I didn't just see all of Florence
I saw the face of the man she fell in love with
Handsome historian of South Carolina State
A man with dreams
Now, a man with a family

There was no doubt in my mind
I was a princess
Princessa tuya papi
Para siempre
Your princess Daddy

Forever

You had no choice but to name me Phil
I was the only child to carry on your father's name
You finally settled on Philadelphia- an empty vessel of the Most High
"Promise me, princess, that you'll name your
first-born son, Phillip.
He'll be the third"

Before leaving for basic training, you said
"You never have to miss me
I am always with you
Whenever you look up at the night sky, thinking of me
Know that I am also looking up thinking of you."
You gave me what every child yearns to have
Your blessing

Even when you lost everything
You lost you
Somehow, you were able to say
"Hasta la muerta, Te Amo"
Until the death, I love you
I love you too, Papi

PHILLIP JOHNSON

PHILADELPHIA

P HILADELPHIA
  Empty vessel of the most high God
Named after the sixth of seven churches in the book of Revelation
To receive a word from God
The city of brotherly love
Upon which, when a slave's foot touches the soil
They are made free

Philadelphia
From Grandma Chizzie's knee
And the sunflower fields of Darlington
To Sojourn like Marcus Garvey
In search of brothers and sisters of Africa in
El Salvador, Portugal, Egypt, Afghanistan, Germany, Oman
London, Spain, Switzerland, France, Japan, Kyrgyzstan

Philadelphia
A door no man can shut

Gateway to Africa
Griot of Jamestown
Channeling the voices of our ancestors
Picking up what was lost
Passing on what is necessary

Philadelphia
Our generation's
Ruth of Bethlehem
Lifting the names of the dead
Harriet on the battlefield
Of the Combahee Ferry Raid
Leading her troops forward

Philadelphia
Picked up a pen
Dared to write her own story
Write her own ticket

Philadelphia
I saw her feet in the fields of Ozatlán
Exploring freely, seemingly without end
I saw her heart in her throat
Descending into Bagram under fire
Muzzle down, rifle loaded and ready
I saw her eyes cast down
Searching the endless stream of caskets
Draped in red, white, and blue,
Looking for answers

Finding none

I saw her legs
Knees high
13 miles into a Thumrait marathon
Refusing to give up
I saw her face smiling once
As her students from all over the world
Raised their right hand and solemnly swore
An oath of allegiance to support and defend
The Constitution and the United States of America
Witnessing the transformation from refugee to citizen
I saw her Pan-African soul
Cry out against the divide separating our people
But I never saw
Philadelphia

TSgt. P. CAROL JOHNSON

MIJO

M IJO
  My son
African Born in Landstuhl, Deutschland, to an American
Deutsch Sprechen
Speaking enough Deutsch to get by in the village

Just a baby in arms, excitedly exploring the Louvre
Sonreindo en Paris atraendo attencion de todo con su hermerso cara
Smiling in Paris, attracting the attention
of everyone with your beautiful face
Mi Principe
My prince
Mijo
My son

Always eager to learn to love
I see you
I see your feet pounding the El Salvadorian earth as you feverously

Pursue the soccer ball
Just three years old

Learning to teach enough English
And speak enough Spanish
Para viver con nuestra gente
To live with our people

Desafiando con valentia los terremotos
Valiantly braving earthquakes
Playing, laughing, dancing, learning, loving

Language did not stop you from sharing your heart with your
Brothers and sisters
On and off the continent of Africa
You learned to speak the language of many lands
Connecting the divide between you and your new family
I see you
Mijo
My son

Racing across the streets of Kensington, London
As though it were your backyard
Around the world and back
Always by my side

And when you weren't
When I had to let you go to Oman and later Afghanistan
You braved your new world without your mother

Mijo
My son
Phillip

Mi socio, mi representante, mi amigo mejor, mi agente, mijo,
My partner, my representative, my agent, my best friend, my son
Mijo
My son
Africa renacio en ti
África was reborn in you

Engineering genius like ancestors past
Capable of creating marvels the world has yet to see
Like the Menes Dam of Egypt
Gannibal's fortress of Kronstadt
Like Anton Wilhelm Amo of your native Deutschland

Your philosophy of the world, having grown all across the globe,
rivals none
With the essence of Ervin James
Transcending slavery to conceive
Jamestown, South Carolina
Fearlessly challenging convention

Mijo
My son
I see you

Te amo hasta el fin de este mundo

La muerte no puede separarnos
Porque estoy adentro de ti
Como tu eres un parte de mi

I love you til the end of this earth
Death cannot separate us because I am in you
Just as you are a part of me
Ich Liebe Dich, Te Amo, I love you
Mijo, my son

PHILLIP

LAZURAH

S OUTHEAST ASIA, WITHIN A war-torn Myanmar
   Amidst military conflicts, the likes of which only Africans have seen
Forced labor camps, executions, political persecution, and
psychological warfare, where sexual violence is another tool of war
Genocide against the Burmese and ethnic minorities is advancing

Of Rose, a star was born
Conceived of the geopolitical intervention of America in Myanmar
Born into violence and chaos
Like other American allies, wives, women, and children cast off
An unacceptable loss

The African child of Nhainse was left behind
To bear the inequity of the father
Marginalized for his African blood and his ethnic Burman roots
The legacy of his father's presence in a foreign land
Somehow, despite facing famine, armed conflict, and displacement
as an outcast among those who were cast out

Your star, Rose
Torn away from your mother's arms
Taken to a new land, a land of opportunity
Only to face a different kind of war on a new Homefront

Cast out by the one who promised to be always faithful
Like your namesake, no death could defeat you
Lazurah arose again
You rise again and again

Triumph in your eyes
Defiance in your spirit
There is no war
No storm is too great for you to survive
I call out to you in the name of our ancestors

Lay claim to our lands
Be the leader our community needs
The man of your home
Resolve yourself to be
Lazurah
Preserve your essence
African
Burmese
American
You too, Sing America

LAZURAH

LEFT BEHIND

O' AFRICA
    Where are thee
Will I ever stand on your lands
Or smell the air off the sea
Or touch a tree
I long for you
Just as I long for my son

Uncle Sam
Took and threw one stone
To knock out one bird
But he got two
One of them was you
Son, you told me
"Ma, they didn't get me like they got those other boys."
But yes
They did
They did

They said no man left behind
But you were
They didn't realize that when they got you
They got me too
Because you are part of me

Now I am out there too
Looking to be found
Until you come back, that part of me is waiting
Waiting to be found
Find that son of mine
I'm just a blue star mom surrounded by blood and tears
Please son
Please son
Stand down

O' Africa, can you heal me?

Deborah Paul

EBONY AND IVORY

L IKE OUR AFRICAN SEAFARING ancestors, navigating
     From freeport to freeport
Up and down the 4142 miles of the Nile River
Out to the Mediterranean Sea
You make countless 3700-mile trips across the continent
First to pull up, willing to drive, until the wheels fall off
To deliver

Home security
Technology
Groceries
A hand, a deck
To deliver our family
Our deliverer
Our Ebony Tree
Economic engine
Like the Great Randolph Phillips

Enfranchising new generations of leaders
A real man
Always faithful
Protecting and providing for our community's most vulnerable
Ebony skin
Just as the majestic Mozambique elephant has evolved
To survive the brutality of the African Ivory trade
You have revolutionized logistics across the continent today
Tomorrow, across the globe
Always in service of the betterment of our beloved community
Our generation's Eli James, son of Ervin James,
who took the mantle to carry forward our legacy
Turn a page on slavery
Walking into freedom as men
Establishing Jamestown, South Carolina

Enterprising
Creating complex physical and metaphysical networks
Mobilizing men
Helping to turn Atlanta into the new Aswan
Ebony and Ivory
Your love gave birth to a Supernova

Como nuestra antepasados
Destrozada en la tormenta
Arrojado en los mares
Las cadenas ni las esclavitud podrian someter el Africano que eres
Tu lucha, tu voluntad, tu dignidad, tu clase

Like our ancestors
Ripped apart in the storm
Tossed on the seas
Shackles nor slavery could subdue the African you are
Your fight, your will, your dignity, your class

You are
Ebony and Ivory

MARCUS, DAMERIA, AND NOVAH PHILLIPS

CAMBRIA HEIGHTS

H<small>OME</small>
    Cars racing by
Subway to the city
Colloquial color, vibrance, you feel in the air
Proud, beautiful black men and women
Standing tall before stately homes

Home
The timber in your voice
The strength of your stride
Arms that never failed to catch her
The knowledge that she would always be there

Home
Land to plant a garden
Decades to water, nurture, and grow together
Meals that never failed to reach the table year after year

Love that brought you home each night
Creating community
Generations of Jameses, Johnsons, Whacks, Phillips, and Scotts
Families that stayed together
Summers and special days spent
In Cambria Heights
Just blocks apart, growing as brother and sister

Cambria Heights
218th St
Jamaica Queens
Linden Blvd
Black
Jamaican
Puerto Rican
Haitian
African
Carvel Ice Cream on Springfield Blvd
City Island celebrations at Sammy's Fishbox

Home
You will always carry with you in your heart
No matter where the world may take you

Dedicated to Eugene Whack

CAMBRIA HEIGHTS

PART III

O' AFRICA: SEGUE TO VOLUME II

ANGEL OF GOD

Angel of God
Zion in her womb
Reborn by God's grace
As He was in the midst
Every step of the way

Knowing that the only thing
Between her children
And total destitution
Was God and her own strength
By the work of her hands
Created a home and a garden
An oasis away from the world

Your arms were our shield
Your faith is our fortress
Your smile is the sunshine on our skin
Though there was no one there to catch you

You never let us fall

We are in awe of your artistry
Mastering the lost art of quilt making
As our enslaved matriarchs intricately
Used a needle and thread to map out the road to freedom
You designed our quilts
So that we would always find our way home

You won't let us miss a moment
Scrapbooking our memories since infancy
Your artwork captures the light
Reflects the lives we want to lead
Your strength is an art

Nursing, caring for, and praying for innumerable patients
Decades prior to the pandemic
At the height of COVID-19
You put your life on the line

Discrimination of any kind
Had no place in your hospital room
The only requirement
That you be a person in need
Your efforts saved lives

Saved souls and changed even the most hardened of hearts
For those who did not make it
You remembered

You grieved
You honored their lives

You are humanity
Our home
Our memories
Our childhood

I lift your name up
Deborah
I praise your pure heart

DEBORAH PAUL

MY AUNT IS AN AKA

D IVINE
    Mine
Thank God and our ancestors
Of one came The Divine Nine
Sisterhoods
Giving life to generations
Of Matriarchs
Healers, accountants, educators, leaders, legislators, and way-makers
Barrier-breaking women who since
1908
Stood
Fearless, proud, and strong
Beautiful grace
In the face of segregation, picket lines, race riots, and integration
Sorors in lock step
Those sisters would keep step
Each and every step ahead
Protecting and building our communities

Our families
Our women

Dignified debutante
Class of '73
With only your legs to carry you
To the courts of one of our sacred
Historically Black Colleges and Universities
To boardrooms around the Americas and Europe
Our Fly Girl
No woman nor man can deny a girl
First in the family CUM LAUDE
Shrewd businesswoman

You know
Dr. Jocelyn Elders said, ***"You can't be what you can't see."***
But I saw you
Eyes sharp and unyielding
Legs unbending
Ready to face any triumph or tragedy
I saw you
Sacrifice without self-interest
Leverage the family home to save our family
Business is business
Without manipulations or stipulations
I saw you, like countless thousands of girls and women saw you
Like me, they were inspired to be the best versions of themselves

It was never about pearls and posturing

Always about the need to achieve
Not for you, but for your brothers
For your sisters, your Sorors

You know
Everybody is asking
Who are these women?
Shattering ceilings
Opening the gates
Who are these women?
On the hill
By the hundreds of thousands
Ascending all around the globe
In Salmon Pink and Apple Green
Who are these women that Dr. Maya Angelou
called her sisters, her Sorors?
These are the women of Alpha Kappa Alpha Sorority Incorporated
And that one
That one is my aunt
My Aunt is an AKA

CAROL DENISE JOHNSON

MRS. SANKOFA

S ANKOFA
Elemental
Mystique
The voice of my ancestors feeding me wisdom

Sankofa
The relief of the wind from the desert sun
Sankofa
The reckoning of the wind's force
The fountain of knowledge
From which life springs forth

A babe I was
When Sankofa took me in her arms
Under her wings
My first cloak of protection

South Carolina

North Vista Elementary
Sankofa prepared me for my first play
"Shoulders high"
"Look me in the eye and tell me"
Exactly, what did Dudley Randall write of W.E.B. and Booker T.?

Middle school
Community Kwanzaa Celebrations
"You can do this, Phee Phee."
"Just a few hundred brothers and sisters
who need to hear what you have to say"

Grown and sophisticated in Germany
Sankofa
Flew halfway around the world to say
"Happy New Year"

Afghanistan
"Come home by any means necessary."
When I came home from Afghanistan
I came home to you
Sankofa

I will always remember
Luxor, Aswan, Cairo, Alexandria, Egypt
Beautiful Nubians
Hand in Karmen's
One foot dipped in the Nile
The other on free land

Eyes up

We knew in that moment
We had achieved our ancestor's wildest dream
The dream of countless generations
Of enslaved Africans
Freed, then subjugated to second-class citizenry
Fighting, scraping, surviving indignity and inhumanity
That one day, a child of theirs might come home
Home
Back to Africa
Back to the bosom of our mother
As free women
Free sisters
Sankofa
Sankofa
Sankofa and I

W. CARMEN HAYNESWORTH

O' AFRICA II

O H AFRICA

Continents away, yet I am closer to you than ever before

Daily, I fly away in my mind

For the first time, the blinders are off

I can see clearly the stars beyond the clouds

Soaring through the fourth dimension of time and space

I see mountain peaks

I yearn to plant my feet

Looking at the acorn on the ground, I see the oak tree it will be

Just as I see the life our love could create in your eyes

From the blade of grass to the oak tree

I am surrounded by life

So little of this life is real

But when I fly away with you in my mind, that time is real

I believe those moments are just moments away

In a blink, my fantasies become reality, and I am conquered

Because you are the sun

Oh Africa
Should I call you Ra
Like the Sun God, you ascended darkness
Resurrected light
Or Horus, son of Osiris and Isis
For after the death of Osiris, you were created
You in his image
Your beauty is a reflection of him
Perhaps Phoenix
No matter how many times life has conquered us
From the flames of Heliopolis, our love is reborn victorious
Or maybe
Like the Egyptian pharaoh
You are the incarnation of God

My greatest fear is a total eclipse of you
How then could I live or grow without your light in my life

Oh Africa
You energize me
Filling me, giving me
All of the serotonin and vitamins I need to be
I wish
Oh, how I wish
I could bottle you
Your eyes, your voice, your wisdom, your strength,
your love, your very breath
So, as I'm euro trippin through eight months of darkness
I could fall into the bottom of the bottle of you

Solar panels, I absorb the rays of your light
Your essence penetrates every layer of me

I am lost in the language of your love
Words cannot describe
The sound of your voice
Your breath on my skin
The feel of your touch
The heat of your body on my cheek
My head on your chest
The beat of your heart
The warmth I feel in your arms
Your hand on my womb

Solo contigo
Me siento mujer
Mi cuerpo
Mi corazon
Mi mente
Mi alma
Solo contigo
Soy libre de ser yo
África, África, África
Te amo
Como el sol para la tierra
Eres mi todo

Only with you
I feel like a woman

My body
My heart
My mind
My soul
Only with you am I free to be me
Africa, Africa, Oh Africa
I love you
Like the sun is to the earth
You are my everything

FROM VERSES TO VISTAS:

A JOURNEY CONTINUES

OUR POETIC COLLECTION HAS been a vessel for emotions, memories, and stories to tell. But now, we delve deeper into the roots and branches of those poetic expressions, transforming them into the rich tapestry of our collective family history.

To be certain, family histories are rarely simple; they branch across generations, rooted in places both remembered and half-forgotten. For the James family, the journey begins with Ervin James—a man born in bondage who forged his legacy by founding Jamestown, South Carolina, in the shadows of Reconstruction. His descendants would grow up in Florence, South Carolina, a city balancing the promise of new beginnings with the heavy hand of the Jim Crow South. In these streets, Black families like the Jameses built their futures, even as the law and social customs conspired to keep them in their place.

To understand the grit and grace that define the James lineage, you have to trace the everyday heroism of women like Chizzie James, navigating a world where Black codes and racial violence were more than distant threats—they were daily realities. It's within this context that the following stories of loss, resilience, and triumph take on their fullest meaning. Connecting the pain of the past with the hope and determination that carried the family forward. To provide proper context within which to better understand – and more rightly, honor – the James lineage, it is appropriate first to fill in some of the boxes, starting with Ervin James himself, the progenitor.

Ervin James stands out as a pivotal figure in the history of Florence County, South Carolina. Born into slavery around 1815 on a plantation near Jamestown, he spent his early years laboring in the fields. He was known among his peers for his quiet strength and unwavering sense of purpose (WMBF News; Green Book of South Carolina). Ervin married Nora James, who is thought to have come from the James Plantation as well. Ervin, one of thirteen siblings, and Nora went on to have fourteen children together.

When the Civil War ended and emancipation came, James saw a rare opportunity. Instead of leaving Jamestown, he chose to build a future there. Not just for himself, but for his family and other newly free people determined to shape their destinies.

In 1870, after years of hard work and saving every possible penny, Ervin James took a remarkable step: he purchased more than 100 acres of land near Mars Bluff. At a time when Black landownership was both rare and often met with hostility, this act was radical and brave (WMBF News; Green Book of South Carolina; SCLiving; GovInfo.gov). James' land soon became the nucleus of a new community for free Black families—Jamestown. It served not only as a farm but also as a sanctuary, gathering place, and the foundation for a thriving Black community.

Under James' leadership, Jamestown grew into a place where education and self-reliance were encouraged. He hosted community gatherings in his home and supported the establishment of the first local Black church,

Bowers Chapel United Methodist, which is still in operation today. Over time, the James family became one of the most respected in the area. Jamestown expanded to over 240 acres between 1870 and 1940, providing land and opportunity for generations of Black families (GovInfo.gov, SCLiving, Bernette Sherman).

Ervin James's legacy endures through his remarkable descendants. Among them are Polly Sheppard, a nationally recognized faith leader and advocate, and Sherlina James, who leads the Jamestown Family Heritage Reunion Committee. Each year, the Jamestown Family reunion draws not only these dedicated leaders but also a vibrant community of professionals and artists, all gathering to honor their shared heritage. (Focus on the Family, 2025).

Today, Jamestown's history is inseparable from the story of Ervin James - a man whose resilience, vision, and belief in the power of land ownership transformed the lives of his family and community. His journey from enslavement to community founder is a story of self-determination and generational strength. His legacy endures as a symbol of hope and perseverance for Black families in the region (HMDB; Bernette Sherman).

Jamestown itself, the city named in honor of this august ancestor, is greatly deserving of our attention. The city traces its roots to the late 1800s and, of course, to its namesake, Ervin James. However, its legacy is inseparable from the history of Black Americans in the South. The area that became Jamestown developed in the shadow of slavery, shaped by the plantation system that dominated the Carolinas. Before emancipation, enslaved Black people in Jamestown endured the same brutal conditions common throughout the region—forced labor in tobacco fields and domestic service, with little hope for freedom or upward mobility. Families were often separated at the whim of enslavers, and the threat of violence was ever-present. Even as some Quaker residents in Guilford County spoke out against slavery and helped operate stops on the Underground Railroad, the institution persisted well into the 19th century (Crow, 1989; Cecelski, 2002).

The Civil War and the abolition of slavery in 1865 marked a turning point, but freedom brought its own challenges. During the era of Reconstruction, Black residents in Jamestown, like those across the South, navigated a world where the promises of liberty were undercut by Black Codes, violence from white supremacist groups, and economic exploitation through sharecropping and tenant farming (Foner, 1988). While some Black families managed to acquire land and build churches and schools, Jim Crow laws soon codified segregation and inequality, restricting opportunities for generations.

Our star character, Ervin James, was one of the most remarkable figures to emerge from this context. He lived through both bondage and freedom and, after emancipation, settled in Jamestown and established roots for his family. The perseverance of Ervin James and those like him was an act of defiance. Through hard work, they managed to purchase land and found the Jamestown community that still bears the family name. The James family cemetery and the stories passed down through descendants stand as testimony to the resilience and endurance of Black people in Jamestown. Their legacy is a reminder that, even in the face of injustice and adversity, Black families like the Jameses built something lasting on Carolina soil (The History of the Jamestown Community, Jamestown News, 2015; Smith, 2008).

One more important, salient point must be brought forward regarding Jamestown. In their masterful exposé entitled ***"Protection, Perseverance, and Power: Landscapes at Jamestown, A Postbellum Black Community in the Pee Dee Region of South Carolina,"*** Christopher

Barton and Terry James explore the history and legacy of Jamestown, a Black community established in the aftermath of the Civil War. The authors focus on how formerly enslaved people used the landscape both as a means of physical protection and as a foundation for building new lives. Through archaeological evidence and oral histories, the article reveals the ways in which the residents of Jamestown transformed their environment. They constructed homes, farms, and communal spaces that reflected their determination to survive and thrive despite the ongoing threats of racial violence and systemic oppression.

Barton and James argue that the landscape of Jamestown became a site of both resistance and empowerment. By examining the community's relationship with the land, the article highlights the strategies residents used to assert autonomy and maintain cultural traditions. The authors show that Jamestown was more than just a place of refuge; it was a testament to the perseverance and agency of Black families carving out a space for themselves in a hostile world. The study ultimately emphasizes the importance of recognizing these historic landscapes as vital sources of Black heritage, resilience, and power. It is undoubtedly the case that the James family played a crucial role in bringing such sterling traits to the fore.

According to the records from the Ervin James Scholarship Fund, the James Family became landowners after the Civil War. Ervin James, determined to provide for his descendants, managed to purchase land—an act of both economic empowerment and social defiance in a state where Black landownership was often met with hostility. It is believed that Ervin James was murdered, possibly in retaliation for purchasing Jamestown, as he disappeared in 1872 without a trace.

As the decades passed, opportunities and pressures drew members of the James family toward Florence. The late 19th and early 20th centuries saw Florence grow rapidly due to the expansion of the railroad and textile industries. Many African American families, including the Jameses, left rural life behind in search of jobs, education, and community resources in the city.

Florence offered better schools and the prospect of economic advancement, though the transition was not without its challenges. The James family, like many others, maintained strong ties to Jamestown—they returned for family reunions, funerals, and celebrations, even as new generations put down roots in Florence.

The migration of the Ervin James family reflects the broader patterns of African American mobility in the South during the post-Reconstruction era: a gradual, determined movement from rural isolation toward the opportunities and networks of urban life.

Before we go further, a few words must be said about the city of Florence, for it was not only host to the James family during their migration but also boasts an illustrious and fascinating history. A brief exploration of its humble beginnings and the role it played in the James family saga is therefore in order.

Florence, South Carolina, sits at the heart of the Pee Dee region and owes its origins to the creation of Florence County in 1888. Before the city's official founding, the area was little more than a crossroads surrounded by pine forests and cotton plantations. The arrival of three major railroads in the mid-19th century transformed this rural landscape into a booming trade and transportation hub. Named after Florence Harllee, the daughter of a railroad executive, the city quickly became a magnet for new residents and businesses (Florence County Historical Society).

In the years after its founding, Florence County's population reflected the broader realities of the post-Reconstruction South. By 1900, African Americans made up roughly 60% of the county's population. Most worked as sharecroppers or tenant farmers in the cotton fields (U.S. Census Bureau, 1900). Economic opportunities brought by the railroads did not erase the legacy of slavery and segregation; Black residents remained confined mainly to the lowest economic rungs, hemmed in by Jim Crow laws and disenfranchisement.

Despite these barriers, Florence's Black community played a vital role in shaping the city's culture and character. Early on, Black residents established churches, schools, and social organizations that became pillars of support and resilience. Black-owned businesses along Dargan Street and in West Florence reflected a drive for autonomy and self-determination in the face of discrimination. These efforts echoed the broader story of Black resilience across the South, where communities found ways to survive - and sometimes thrive - even within a system designed to keep them marginalized (South Carolina African American Heritage Commission).

The story of Ervin James and his involvement in both the development of Florence and of the generations that followed him is truly remarkable. Over the decades, James's descendants maintained and expanded the family's holdings, contributing to Florence's cultural and economic development. Their history has been celebrated locally, primarily through the preservation of the James family cemetery and the recognition of their land as a symbol of Black self-determination (South Carolina State Historic Preservation Office: African American Historic Places).

Florence's story is inseparable from the story of the South itself: a landscape marked by struggle and transformation. The city's founding, its demographic shifts, and the enduring influence of its Black residents all offer a window into the larger narrative of race, progress, and identity in the region. Today, the legacy of Ervin James and his family stands as a testament to Florence's complex history. In this place, the resilience of African Americans helped shape the community's character and continues to inspire both scholarly research and public commemoration. The ability, however, for African Americans to truly branch out and make inroads into the American social landscape was limited and often met with great resistance, as we shall now see.

A widely known stain on the American landscape – one that ferociously and harshly impacted the lives of Blacks in the South, was the institution of the Jim Crow laws. The introduction of these laws marked a period of systematic indignity, violence, and disenfranchisement for African Americans. After the collapse of Reconstruction in 1877, white lawmakers swiftly moved to codify racial segregation and white supremacy through a patchwork of state and local statutes. These laws, known as "Jim Crow," mandated separate schools, transportation, restrooms, and even cemeteries for Black and white citizens. The intent was clear: to reassert social control over Black people and reverse the gains made during the brief window of Reconstruction (Woodward, 1955).

Before the formalization of Jim Crow, Southern states enacted Black Codes - laws that tightly restricted the freedom of newly emancipated African Americans. For instance, Mississippi's Black Code of 1865 required Black laborers to sign yearly labor contracts; those who refused could be arrested and forced into unpaid labor (Foner, 1988). In South Carolina, Black people were prohibited from holding certain occupations unless they paid a hefty annual tax. Vagrancy laws enabled law enforcement to round up unemployed Black men and lease them out to plantations. These practices were precursors to the later, more comprehensive Jim Crow regime.

The consequences of these laws were devastating. In Plessy v. Ferguson (1896), the Supreme Court infamously upheld the constitutionality of racial segregation under the doctrine of *"separate but equal,"* legitimizing Jim Crow nationwide. The reality was far from equal - schools for Black children were chronically underfunded, and public facilities were often little more than shacks. Black citizens who attempted to challenge these injustices risked violence, arrest, or even lynching. In 1898 alone, an estimated 123 African Americans were lynched, most in the South, often for minor *"offenses"* against the racial order (Equal Justice Initiative, 2017).

These indignities were not just abstract policies - they shaped and scarred individual families, including that of Ervin James. He was forced to navigate a world where Black Codes and Jim Crow laws dictated nearly every aspect of life. After emancipation, his and his family's attempts to build independent lives - purchasing land, founding churches, and striving for education – met with relentless obstacles: discriminatory laws blocked voting rights, limited economic opportunities, and subjected them to constant threat of state-sanctioned violence.

In the 1960s, Florence, South Carolina, was a place of hard lessons and quiet bravery, especially for Black families trying to make a life out of what little was left to them. The James family's neighborhood was stitched together by stories, front porches, and the kind of work that left your hands cracked but your spirit, somehow, unbroken.

Segregation was not just the law; it was the air you breathed - thick, ever-present, shaping every corner store and schoolhouse. The working-class Black communities in Florence were circled by railroad tracks, both a boundary and a lifeline. Many men, including my forefathers, took shifts at the Seaboard Coast Line, coming home bone-tired, uniforms streaked with oil, pockets often empty, but heads held high. Their women kept boarders, took in laundry, and moved through town with a kind of grace that belied the daily humiliations they endured. *"We had to make a way out of no way,"* was a common refrain found in so many Black Southern homes (Wilkerson, 2010).

There was a hush when outsiders passed and a lively hum when neighbors gathered - Sunday mornings radiated with gospel and the scent of fried catfish. Under the surface, tension simmered. Florence, like much of the South, was slow to change. When the Civil Rights Movement reached its streets, it was both a hope and a risk. Historian Charles M. Payne writes that **_"ordinary people... took extraordinary risks"_** just by attending a mass meeting or trying to register to vote (Payne, 1995). Edmond, Chizzie, and their adult children were all registered voters. The James family, like so many others, measured their days in small victories – another week with the property taxes paid, another night with everyone safe at home.

Despite the barriers mentioned, the James family persevered, laying the foundations for future generations. Their experiences reflect the broader struggle of African Americans to assert dignity and claim their rights in the face of legalized oppression. The story of Ervin James is a testament to resilience, but also a reminder of the daily humiliations and hardships imposed by the Jim Crow system - a system designed to keep Black families like his in perpetual subjugation (James, 2020).

The story of the Ervin James family is more than a series of names and dates—it's a living inheritance. An inheritance that's shaped by resilience, quiet triumphs, and the kind of strength that only reveals itself over generations. Understanding where the family has come from gives context to the lives they built. Still, it's in the personal details - meals shared, stories whispered on porches, the rhythm of daily life, and especially the often triumphant and sometimes tragic events that at times brought the family together and, other times, threatened to tear it apart - that their legacy truly comes alive.

With this foundation in mind, we turn from the broad strokes of history to the close-up view: an intimate family biography, rich with memory and meaning. Here, the focus shifts from the events that shaped the James family to the people who made those moments matter - their hopes, their heartbreaks, and the ways they found joy, even in the hardest seasons.

It was on July 4th, 1969, in Florence, South Carolina, that Carol Johnson heard the commotion. Just twelve years old, and she had already learned the life and death necessity of situational awareness. Another domestic dispute, another day in her life since her father, Phillip Johnson, passed away. But something about this fight seemed different. ***"Give me the gun, fool, give me the damn gun, fool."*** Boom! No sooner than those words were spoken, a single shot was fired, taking with it sparkling eyes, the most disarming smile, the face, and the life of the most beautiful woman in her world, her mother, Baby Ruth.

Carol didn't have time to cry, to feel, and certainly not to grieve. Never looking back, she grabbed her brothers and headed to Grandma Chizzie's house. Later, Carol and her siblings all moved into the family home of the late Phillip and Ruth Johnson. As Ruth James Johnson was laid to rest, the matriarch inside of Carol Denise Johnson was born.

Although the loss of Baby Ruth devastated the entire family, Carol understood that struggle, loss, and devastation were all a part of life. The James family was born of that struggle. As Carol reflected on her family and her rock, Grandma Chizzie, she understood her place and her great responsibility to the family.

Grandma Chizzie was the great-granddaughter of Ervin James. Born in 1904, Chizzie James was raised at the height of Jim Crow and Ku Klux Klan violence. Chizzie married Edmond James at a relatively young age. She was one of eleven siblings, and although she shared a close bond with all of them, Savannah, Jasper, and Robert visited most frequently. Their children spent much of their childhood together and grew up side by side.

Chizzie raised chickens, grew flowers and vegetables, bartered and sold poultry, eggs, pies, and other baked goods to relieve financial pressures in the household. Budgeting to a science, Grandma Chizzie made sure that taxes and other critical bills were paid. She raised her girls to fear God. Despite her own thwarted academic achievement, she ensured education and life skills were a primary focus for all four of her girls.

The city of Florence was founded in Florence County. The county of Florence and the rural communities and folks pre-existed the city, which brought many modern advances. Black folks of the day developed their own infrastructure and depended on each other to maintain Black schools, hospitals, and other segregated public spaces of the time. Children grew up learning a variety of crafts and trade skills in their homes. Most of the country at this time did not have any public black high schools. Hines, a history researcher, points out that, *"In 1915, not one black public high school existed in 23 southern cities with populations of more than 20,000, including Tampa, New Orleans, Charleston, and Charlotte."* (Hines et al., 2011, p. 384) However, Florence boasted Wilson School, established in 1869 by the Freedman's Bureau at the end of the Civil War (The Historical Mark Database, 2023). In fact, Wilson High is one of the few secondary educational institutions established by the Freedman's Bureau still in operation today, though not in its original building. It was Wilson High School students who, on March 3rd through 4th, marched from Trinity Baptist Church to the Kress Store to stage a sit-in where they were arrested.(Green Book of South Carolina) The young James family benefited from the rigors offered at Wilson High. All four girls would be educated at good ol' Wilson High. Ruth James even played basketball.

Later in life, Edmond would fall ill with heart disease and high blood pressure. Chizzie and her girls took care of him in his final years, up until his death at the age of 55. To continue to provide for her family after Edmond James passed away, Miss Chizzie ran the numbers. This meant that anyone in the community who wanted to play the numbers would see Miss Chizzie. She also brewed good homemade wine and moonshine, selling to both White and Black customers without discrimination.

Ms. Chizzie's twin daughters, Mary and Martha James, were inducted into the Wilson High School alumni association. Martha then attended Benedict College. The twins both relocated north, finally settling in New York and building careers at Macy's in New York City, where they remained for over forty years. Macy's provided both women with the opportunity to support not only their children but also their many nieces and nephews, including Carol, whom they both regarded as a daughter. They regularly shopped for themselves and the family at Macy's, taking advantage of their employee discounts. Both women maintained extensive wardrobes, setting a standard for high fashion in the family. Ruth and Edna Mae stayed in Florence. Neither Edna Mae nor Baby Ruth would live past their 35th birthdays. Edna Mae became very ill and struggled with complications from bronchitis and pneumonia, leading to her death in 1968.

In 1954, Baby Ruth met the love of her life, Phillip Johnson, a Korean War Veteran who served in the 82nd Airborne Division. They married and had three children. Tragically, Ruth witnessed Phillip's death in 1959 and did not fully recover from the loss and grief. Ruth's youngest, Phillip, went to live with Chizzie as a newborn. Instead of traveling the world with her husband and raising her children as military brats, Ruth buried her husband and her dreams with him. Tragically, Baby Ruth was set on a path that led to her getting involved with a violent man, one who would eventually take her life.

On the 4th of July 1969, it was Chizzie James who laid a white sheet over her daughter's body so that no one would see what ultimately became of her beautiful face. When the dust of death settled, Chizzie was left with three more orphaned grandchildren to raise. Phillip was only nine years old at the time of Ruth's death. Grandma Chizzie was older, and Carol sensed that she could only do so much.

During Grandma Chizzie's and Carol's only grocery shopping trip together in downtown Florence, Carol once witnessed the disregard and blatant disrespect with which her grandmother was being treated. Disgusted, she heard Grandma assume a lowly, subservient position as she interacted with a young White salesclerk. *"Here you go, ma'am. Yes ma'am. Thank you, ma'am."* For Carol, this action did not match the high regard and respect with which Grandma Chizzie was held in the community of her people.

"Grandma! Why are you calling her ma'am?" Carol asked. *"She should be calling you ma'am!"* *"Shh, just hush,"* Grandma Chizzie replied.

Carol was beginning to learn about the expectation of acquiescence that came with her social identity. African Americans were not in a position to question the hostile status quo that characterized the unequal racial dynamics of the time. Although the violence of Jim Crow had weakened, it had not yet died, so Grandma Chizzie had to be cautious in interacting with the young, White clerk. Carol never forgot that incident, but it was one of many that were beyond her control.

Never again! Carol resolved within herself. She wanted to defend her aging grandmother and shelter her from the storm of racism. *"Never again will I watch Grandma Chizzie shuffle off the sidewalk for a White passerby. Never again will I listen to my grandmother say 'Yes, ma'am' to a White young salesclerk staring at her feet. Never again will I allow my grandmother to have to expose herself to any more abuses."* From this day forward, Carol vowed to herself, *"I will do the grocery shopping for the house. I will go to downtown Florence to pay the bills. I will make sure that my brothers are taken care of. When I do go out, I will get my due respect!"* It was there, during her formative years, that Carol developed a fearlessness and backbone that would stay with her the rest of her life. There would be no challenge too great, because Carol had already experienced the worst day of her life. If that didn't break her, then nothing would.

Taking no prisoners in the community, Carol dominated on the basketball court. Just like her mother Ruth, she played basketball for good ol' Wilson High in Florence, S.C. Playing against the best male ball players in Florence in backyard courts and community parks, the girls competing against Carol stood no chance.

Carol played varsity girls' basketball up until she graduated. Prior to graduating, she also had an opportunity very few young ladies of color could achieve in the United States, which was to make her debut in the Darlington Debutante Ball. This highly prestigious and longstanding event was a coming-of-age tradition that celebrated young women making their debut into society. It typically took place during the winter season, providing an opportunity for young women to be formally presented to society in an indoor setting. The debutantes were introduced to attendees in elegant white ball gowns, carrying hand-tied nosegays of flowers. Carol was acutely aware that Black debutante balls in the American South—especially in the Carolinas—were exceedingly rare in the mid-1900s. While white debutante traditions had long flourished as a way to introduce young women to elite society, Black communities faced persistent institutional and social barriers that made such rituals largely inaccessible. For Carol, then, this opportunity held tremendous significance.

Late Phillip Johnson's sisters took the lead in ensuring that Carol was prepared for that special day. Raising money throughout the family, Rosa Wingate took out a half-page advertisement to promote Carol's selection.

Her aunts, Joanne and Carolyn, were also involved in the preparations. Carol learned many valuable skills at her debut, brushing shoulders with other up-and-coming young ladies and young men of color. She developed confidence and poise that would always set her apart from her peers. Decades later, Carol would reflect on how meaningful this experience was in her life, *"It was one of the best milestones of my life. It didn't only shine the light on what's to come for a girl growing into womanhood. That event also emphasized grace, tradition, family, and community ties. It provided me with an opportunity to participate in a formal social occasion and create lasting memories!"* Carol had no way of knowing then that she would one day be the one organizing countless philanthropic benefits and cultural events for the community.

Finishing Wilson High with good grades and athletic ability, Carol had the opportunity to attend any university of her choosing. Through Phillip Johnson's service and tragic death in the United States Army, a legacy of provision for her education afforded her the tuition and financial resources she needed to go to college. Carol would receive the Dependent Education Assistance benefit through the Veterans Affairs Administration. At the time, this benefit covered the full cost of tuition and fees. When the time came, Carol's choice of college was unsurprisingly reflective of her upbringing, her unapologetic love for her people, and her history. She understood the value of the education she had received at Wilson High, and that a historically Black college or university could do even more to prepare her for the world awaiting her. It was with great pride that she chose to attend South Carolina State University in Orangeburg, S.C., home of the Bulldogs.

As the years turned over and the world shifted, the story of Ervin James and his kin became something more than a family's private memory. From the red clay fields where Ervin first staked his claim, to the crowded porches and backroads of towns marked by both hope and ruin, the James family carved out a life against odds that never fully relented. Their homes—weathered cabins, tenant shacks, finally brick and clapboard houses—stood as quiet witnesses to an unbroken line of resilience. They moved when forced, stayed when they could, always binding themselves to neighbors, churches, and the struggles of the segregated South. Through every hardship, they found ways to hold on to dignity, faith, and each other. It was this inheritance—a legacy written not just in land or name, but in the stubborn will to survive and reach higher—that carried forward. And so, as the weight of the past pressed on, it was not just Ervin's shadow but his steady strength that watched over Carol Johnson, guiding her steps as she stood on the threshold of a future her ancestors could scarcely imagine.

PHILLIP JOHNSON

RUTH JAMES JOHNSON

ON TO VOLUME II:

A MATRIARCH'S LEGACY

A S WE CLOSE THE pages of this poetic journey, we pause to honor a guiding light, my aunt Carol, the matriarch whose life's tapestry was woven with resilience and grace. Her spirit, a beacon through our family's history, now beckons us forward into a new narrative. The verses here have been whispers of her influence, and it is her remarkable odyssey that will unfold in the narrative-driven memoir to come.

This next volume is a respectful nod to Aunt Carol's impact on our family. It stands as a testament to her enduring legacy, a singular chronicle of a life that shaped our own.

Join me as we transition from the poetry of collective memory to the prose of her extraordinary story and celebrate the life of a woman whose presence was a gift to us all and to thousands of girls and women.

ACKNOWLEDGMENTS

I AM ETERNALLY GRATEFUL to my ancestors who have passed on to be with our Lord. Ervin James, who, in 1870, following the devastation of slavery, worked with his siblings and children to buy a settlement establishing Jamestown, South Carolina. Your legacy changed the course of history for African Americans in the South and my life. His great-granddaughter and my great-great-grandmother, Chizzie James, was a humble baker who shepherded four generations through the struggles of life. Grandma Chizzie, despite being eighty when I was born, raised me until her death. Grandma Chizzie instilled in me who I am, where I am, and where I came from, and who we are as a people. To my living ancestors, I am so blessed and privileged for their influence and life lessons. My grandaunt, Carolyn Johnson, my granduncle Albert *"Sonny"* Johnson, and Aunt Hatti Smith, I love you.

My mother, Deborah Paul, who gave me life, raised me, and has remained by my side through it all. Your service in the medical community, saving and extending lives for over 40 years, has positively changed the lives of countless people. You taught me to cook, and to love God and myself.

I love you, Mommy. Phillip Johnson, my daddy, your unconditional love and support have been a grounding force in my life.

Marcus Phillips, brother of mine, I could not have done this without your support. The James legacy lives on with you. To Karmen Haynesworth, my sister and very first teacher, your inspiration shaped my life. To my veteran and soul sister, Danielle Wilder, together we served in the United States Air Force, engaging in battles all over the world on behalf of this country. Thank you for always having my six. Lazurah, you stole my heart from the first. Your strength and compassion are an inspiration to me and so many others. You have completed our family.

Little Phillip, you are my heart, my best friend, and my anchor. Watching you grow and growing with you as we traveled and built our life together has been my greatest honor.

I would like to thank Melody Marie Luciano Norris of Black Cat Sweeps LLC DBA Black Cat Studios; your diligent efforts in copy editing and formatting have made all of the difference.

Dr. Lindelwa Ntutela, your friendship and steady support over the years pushed me to keep moving forward. Thank you for always championing *O' Africa Poetry*.

Special Thanks to the Jamestown Family Reunion Committee and the Summerville Legacy Commission. Your works ensure that Ervin James' legacy lives on.

AUTHOR'S NOTE

O' AFRICA IS MY love letter to Africa and my Pan-African family. This collection of poems was written over the past 20 years. It reflects my journey with my brothers and sisters on and off the continent of Africa, as well as across the globe. As a Pan-African, I believe it is necessary to break down barriers of language and cultural differences separating our people. African unity is the only path forward.

stay in touch
www.oafricapoetry.com

ABOUT THE AUTHOR

Philesha Carol Johnson is a multifaceted individual, embodying roles as a mother, writer, and advocate for transformation and triumph through self-discovery, particularly within the context of African American identity and the Pan African diaspora. As a human services professional and United States Air Force Veteran, Carol boasts over two decades of dedicated research, speaking engagements, and written contributions in the realm of expressive arts. Her academic achievements include a Master's Degree in Human Relations, where she was honored with Summa Cum Laude distinction from the University of Oklahoma, and a Bachelor of Arts in English and Literature from Southern New Hampshire University. She pursued further academic endeavors as a Doctoral Candidate in Adult Learning at the University of Connecticut.

Having traversed diverse terrains, both geographically and intellectually, Carol's journey has seen her train peer airmen across Europe and the Middle East, delving into the intricacies of adult learning, and uncovering the vulnerabilities shared by her clients. Fluent in Spanish, she has embraced the richness of cultural exchange and linguistic diversity.

Carol's affinity for expressive arts traces back to her earliest memories, where she took the stage before Kwanzaa audiences at the tender age of five, laying the foundation for a lifelong passion. Today, she resides and operates from her home base in Connecticut, balancing her professional pursuits with the joys and responsibilities of being a devoted football mom to her two sons. The publication of her poetry collection stands as a testament to her unwavering commitment to realizing her dreams and sharing her creative voice with the world.

BIBLIOGRAPHY

CROW, JEFFREY J. *A History of African Americans in North Carolina*. North Carolina Office of Archives and History, 1989.

Cecelski, David S. *The Waterman's Song: Slavery and Freedom in Maritime North Carolina*. University of North Carolina Press, 2002.

Equal Justice Initiative. "Lynching in America: Confronting the Legacy of Racial Terror." 2017.

Florence County Historical Society. "History of Florence County."

Florence County Museum. "The Ervin James Family."

Foner, Eric. *Reconstruction: America's Unfinished Revolution, 1863–1877*. Harper & Row, 1988.

Green Book of South Carolina. "Civil Rights Sit-Ins in Florence, S.C" Accessed July 16, 2025. https://greenbookofsc.com/locations/civil-rights-sit-ins-in-florence-sc/

Green Book of South Carolina. "Historic Jamestown Community." Accessed July 16, 2025.

Hine, Darlene Clark, et al. *African American Odyssey*. Pearson, 2013.

Hines, Darlene Clark, et al. 2011, p. 384.

HMDB (Historical Marker Database). "Jamestown Community and the James Family." Accessed July 16, 2025.

James, Vivian M. *The Ervin James Family: A History of Faith, Family, and Freedom*. 2020.

Payne, Charles M. *I've Got the Light of Freedom: The Organizing Tradition and the Mississippi Freedom Struggle*. University of California Press, 1995.

SCLiving. Sherman, Bernet. "Legacy of Land: Jamestown's Founding Families." *SC Living Magazine*, February 2022.

Sherman, Bernet. "The James Family of Jamestown." In *South Carolina Heritage Series*, vol. 15, 2021.

Smith, Charles W. "Ervin James and the Founding of Jamestown's Black Community." *Carolina Heritage*, 2008.

South Carolina African American Heritage Commission. *African American Historic Places in South Carolina*.

South Carolina Encyclopedia. "Florence County."

South Carolina State Historic Preservation Office. "African American Historic Places."

Strauss, William, and Neil Howe. *The Fourth Turning: An American Prophecy*. First trade paperback edition, Broadway Books, 1998.

The Historical Marker Database, 2023.

"The History of Jamestown, South Carolina (Florence County)."

"The History of the Jamestown Community." *Jamestown News*, April 2015.

U.S. Census Bureau. *Twelfth Census of the United States, 1900*.

Wilkerson, Isabel. *The Warmth of Other Suns: The Epic Story of America's Great Migration*. New York: Random House, 2010.

WMBF News. "A Piece of History: The Ervin James Story." Accessed July 16, 2025.

GovInfo. "Reconstruction Era: South Carolina's Black Landowners." U.S. Government Publishing Office. Accessed July 16, 2025.

Ervin James Scholarship Fund. "The Family History."

www.ingramcontent.com/pod-product-compliance
Lightning Source LLC
Chambersburg PA
CBHW051531120626
46551CB00012B/1170